MAKE BELIEVE STORIES: THE STORY OF A WHITE ROCKING HORSE

BY LAURA LEE HOPE

[ZHINGOORA BOOKS]

This edition is published by
Zhingoora Books.

The Cover is Designed by Pallav Sethiya.

CONTENTS

CHAPTER

CHAPTER I

READY FOR A RACE

One by one the lights went out. One by one the shoppers left the toy department of the store. One by one the clerks rode down in the elevators. At last all was still and quiet and dark—that is, all dark except for a small light, so the night-watchman could see his way around.

"Now we can have some fun!" cried a voice, and it seemed to come from a Calico Clown, lying down in a box next to a Bold Tin Soldier. "Now we can really be ourselves, and talk and move about."

"We can, if we are sure there is no one to watch us," bleated a Lamb on Wheels, who stood on the floor near a White Rocking Horse. "You know, as well as I do, Calico Clown, that we cannot do as we please if there are any eyes watching us," said the Lamb.

"No one can see us," said the Bold Tin Soldier. "I am glad the clerks and shoppers are gone. It will be some time before the watchman comes up here, and my men and I will be glad to move about. All ready there!" he called to his soldiers, for he was captain over a brave company of tin warriors. "Attention! Stand up straight and get ready to march! You have been in your box all day, and now it is time to come out!"

It was true; the Bold Tin Soldier and his men had been in a box on the toy counter all day. For, as you have been told, the playthings cannot make believe come to life nor move about when any human eyes are watching them. They must wait until they are alone, which is generally after dark. That is why you have never seen your doll or your rocking horse moving about by itself.

But now, in the toy store, from which every one had gone, some strange things happened. The Calico Clown stood up near the Candy Rabbit and looked about. Then the Calico Clown banged together the shiny brass cymbals he held in his hands.

"Clang! Bang!" went the cymbals.

"Ha! that sounds like war," cried the Bold Tin Soldier. "Come, my men!
Forward—march!"

And then and there the tin soldiers, with their captain holding his shiny tin sword in his hand, marched out of their box and around the toy counter of the big department store.

Yes, I wish you could have seen them; but it isn't allowed, you know. Just the very minute the eyes of a boy or a girl, or, for that matter, a father or mother or aunt, uncle or cousin—just the very moment any one looks, the toys are as still as clothespins.

"Aren't they fine?" cried a Monkey on a Stick, as he scrambled up to the very top of his staff, so he might look over the pile of building blocks that stood near some picture books. "I wish I were a soldier!"

"Oh, no!" exclaimed a Boy Doll.

"You are funnier as a Monkey," remarked the Calico Clown.

"But I am not as funny as you are," laughed the Monkey. "Tell us a joke, that's a good fellow! Tell us something funny, Calico Clown, so we may laugh. We have had no fun all day."

"All right," agreed the Calico Clown, with a smile, as he softly banged his cymbals together. "I'll see if I can think of a joke."

The Bold Tin Soldier and his men stopped marching to listen to what the Calico Clown might say. The Candy Rabbit raised his big ears up straighter, so that he would miss nothing. The Lamb on Wheels gave herself a shake, seemingly so the kinks would come out of her woolly coat, and the Monkey on a Stick swung by his tail.

"Yes, I'll tell you a joke," said the Calico Clown. "It is a sort of riddle. Listen, and see if any of you can answer it."

"The Sawdust Doll was very clever at answering riddles," said the Bold
Tin Soldier. "I wish she were here now."

"But she isn't," said the Candy Rabbit. "I liked that Sawdust Doll very much, but she has gone away."

"Yes, some lady bought her for a little girl's birthday," came from the Monkey on a Stick. "You are right, Tin Soldier, that doll was very clever at answering the riddles the Clown used to ask."

"Well, if you don't all stop talking now, how am I going to tell this joke?" asked the Calico Clown crossly. "Now, who is a—"

"I wonder if the Sawdust Doll will come back and see us once again, as she did before?" asked the Lamb on Wheels, not paying much attention to what the Calico Clown said. "Don't you remember, Tin Soldier, how she once came back to us, after she had been sold and taken away?"

"Clang! Bang!" went the cymbals of the Calico Clown.

"What's the matter?" asked the Monkey on a Stick.

"Matter? Matter enough, I should say!" replied the Clown. "Here I am asked to tell a funny joke, and none of you will listen. You keep on talking about the Sawdust Doll. I liked her as much as any one. But she is gone—she was sold away from us. To-morrow some of us may be sold, and never see the others again. Let's be gay and jolly while we can!"

"That's what I say!" exclaimed the Candy Rabbit. "Really, we are not very polite to go on talking when the Calico Clown wants to amuse us with one of his famous jokes. We should listen to him."

"You are right!" cried the Bold Tin Soldier. "Come now," he went on, as he waved his sword over his head, "I do not want to be cross with you, my toy friends, but I command silence! Silence while the Calico Clown tells his joke!"

The toys on the counters and shelves settled down and turned their eyes toward the Clown in his funny calico suit of many colors.

"I'm sure you will all laugh at this joke!" cried the Calico Clown. "It is so funny I have to laugh myself whenever I tell it. Thank you for getting them quiet so they can listen to me, Bold Tin Soldier. I am glad you are a friend—"

"Say, you'd better tell that joke, if you're going to!" broke in the captain. "I don't know how long they'll stay quiet. And I want to march around some more before morning comes and we have to stay in our box all day. You know it is the Christmas season, and any one of us may be bought any day and taken far off. So let us be jolly together while we may. All quiet now, for the Calico Clown's joke!"

"Thank you," returned the funny fellow again. "Now, why is it that when—"

And just then there was a rumbling, rolling sound on the floor of the toy department.

"Dear me!" exclaimed the Candy Rabbit, "can that be the watchman coming so soon?"

They all listened, and heard the noise more plainly. It rumbled and rolled nearer and nearer.

"Dear me!" said the Calico Clown, "I'm never going to get a chance to tell my joke. What is it, Candy Rabbit? Can you see?"

The sweet chap was just going to say he could see nothing, when there came a whinny from a big White Rocking Horse standing on the floor near a lawn swing.

"Oh, you're here at last, are you?" neighed the White Rocking Horse.

"Yes, I'm here," answered a voice, and with it came again the rumbling, rolling sound. "I'm sorry if I am late, but I had to go over in the sporting goods section to get a pair to fit me."

"A pair of what to fit who? Who is it?" asked the Monkey on a Stick, for he had taken a seat behind a pile of building blocks, and could not see very well.

"What's going on here, anyhow?" he asked, as he began to climb up to the top of his stick.

Then all the toys looked at the White Rocking Horse, and they saw, trundling toward him, an Elephant on roller skates.

"Oh, how funny he looks!" laughed the Calico Clown. "Oh, dear me! This is better than any joke I could tell! Oh, how funny!" And the Calico Clown doubled up in such a kink of laughter that his cymbals tinkled again and again.

"What is so funny?" asked the Elephant on roller skates.

"You are," replied the Clown. "Of course we are glad to see you," he added. "And please excuse me for laughing at you. But, really, I cannot help it! You do look so funny! I—I never saw an elephant on roller skates before."

"And I never before was on roller skates," answered the toy Elephant. "I don't believe I'll ever put them on again, either," he said. "But when the White Rocking Horse asked me to race with him, that was the only way I could think of to make it fair, as he is so much faster than I. He said I might put anything I liked on my feet."

9

"What's this? What's this?" cried the Bold Tin Soldier. "Is there to be a race between an Elephant on roller skates and the White Rocking Horse?"

"Yes," answered the Horse himself, "we are going to have a little race, just for fun, you know. I thought it would be amusing."

"Where are you going to run the race?" asked the Candy Rabbit.

"Down to the elevators and back again," answered the White Rocking Horse. "You see, my friends, it came about in this way," he explained. "The Elephant was always telling how fast he could run. He said the real elephants in the jungle, after whom he is patterned, were swifter than horses. I said I did not think so. I told him I could beat him in a race, so we agreed to try it some night. I said he could put on roller skates if he wished, since I had rockers, like those of a chair, fastened on my hoofs."

The White Rocking Horse was a proud fellow, with his long tail and mane of real hair. Proudly he held up his head. Proudly he rocked to and fro. On his back was a red saddle of real leather.

"Get ready for the race!" called the Calico Clown, clanging his cymbals. "This will be real, jolly fun! Ready for the race!"

The Horse and Elephant stood on a line, which was a crack in the floor, and they were just going to rush toward the elevators when, all of a sudden, the Candy Rabbit cried:

"Hush!"

CHAPTER II

THE RUDE BOY

Suddenly all the toys, who had been crowding to the edges of the shelves and counters to watch the race between the Horse and the Elephant, became very quiet. The Candy Rabbit seemed to shrink down behind the Monkey on a Stick. The Bold Tin Soldier slipped his sword back into its scabbard, and his men lowered their guns. The Calico Clown, who had been about to bang his cymbals together, dropped them to his sides. The Lamb on Wheels, who had just been going to ask a Rag Doll if she did not want to get up on her back, so she might see better, rolled herself under the counter, and the White Rocking Horse and the Elephant on his roller skates looked around in surprise.

"What's the matter?" neighed the Horse. "Why did you call out for us to hush, Candy Rabbit?"

"I thought I heard a noise," was the answer. "Maybe the night watchman is coming. If he is, he must never see us at our play. Something dreadful would happen, if he did."

"Hush! Not so loud!" whispered the Calico Clown. "What you say is very true, Candy Rabbit. We dare not move about or talk if we are looked at by human eyes. But I do not think the watchman is coming."

"How can we be sure the watchman is not looking at us?" whispered the Monkey on a Stick." I'd like to see this race."

"So would I," said the Calico Clown. "And there is only one way we can be certain the watchman is not here."

"Tell us how!" suggested the Bold Tin Soldier.

"This is the way," answered the Calico Clown. "I will recite that funny riddle I started to give you earlier in the evening. If the watchman is here he will laugh at it, and then we'll know he is watching us."

"That will be a fine way!" said the Lamb on Wheels. "Go ahead, Calico Clown. Tell us the riddle, and we must all listen to see if the watchman laughs."

"All right! Here I go!" agreed the Calico Clown. He banged his cymbals together and then, in a loud voice, asked: "Why is a basket of soap bubbles like a piece of chocolate cake?"

They all listened after the Calico Clown had asked this riddle. But there was no laugh. It was as quiet in the toy department as if none of the playthings had made believe come to life.

"I guess the watchman isn't there," said the Calico Clown, "or else he would have laughed at my riddle."

"Maybe he is waiting for the answer," said the White Rocking Horse. "I think that must be it, for I don't see anything very funny in the riddle itself. Maybe the watchman is waiting for you to give the answer, and then he'll laugh."

"Oh, I'm sure that is it," said the Elephant. "Go ahead, Calico Clown! Tell us the answer! Why is a basket of soap bubbles like a piece of chocolate cake? If we hear that, maybe we'll laugh, as well as the watchman. What's the answer?"

"That's the funny part of it!" said the Calico Clown. "There is no answer."

"No answer!" cried the White Rocking Horse. "That's a funny riddle!"

"I knew you'd think it was funny," returned the Calico Clown. "That is why I tried so hard to tell it earlier in the evening, to make you all jolly. No, there really is no answer. I don't believe a basket full of soap bubbles is a bit like a piece of chocolate cake. But I just thought I'd ask to see if any of you knew."

He waited a moment, but none of the toys answered.

"And the watchman doesn't seem to know, either," said the Monkey on a Stick. "I guess he can't be here, or he would have laughed, Mr. Calico Clown."

"I'm sure he would," said the joking chap. "It must be all right. No one is looking at us. On with the race!"

"Yes," rumbled the Elephant, away deep down in his trunk, "if we are going to have this race let's get it over with. I must go back to my place among the camels and lions and tigers before morning."

The Elephant, who had borrowed a pair of roller skates to race with the White Rocking Horse, lived in a large Noah's Ark with the other animals from the jungle and the desert.

"Get ready now!" cried the Bold Tin Soldier. "On your marks, Horse and Elephant! I will have one of my men fire his gun as a signal to start the race!"

"Good!" neighed the White Rocking Horse.

Slowly he began to sway back and forth, while the Elephant slid along on his roller skates until both animals stood, once more, on the crack in the floor. When the Candy Rabbit had cried "Hush!" they had both slid back toward the toy counter. Later on the make-believe folk found that the noise was caused by a Jack in the Box springing up quickly to watch the race.

"Bang!" went a toy pop gun. And then the race began!

And such a race as it was! Across the floor, toward the elevators, went the Elephant, gliding along on the roller skates. Back and forth swayed the Rocking Horse, and each time he moved he went a little faster. His tail and mane streamed out in the air and his red saddle of real leather glistened in the light of the one dim electric lamp.

"The Elephant is winning! The Elephant is winning!" cried the Monkey on a Stick. He rather favored the Elephant, for, like the big chap, the Monkey also had come from a jungle.

"The Horse is going faster!" cried the Bold Tin Soldier. "I'm sure the Horse will win the race!" The Tin Captain rather favored the Horse, since all soldiers like horses.

"It is too soon, yet, to tell who will win," remarked the Calico Clown. "They have to go to the elevators and come back to the starting mark—the crack in the floor—before the race is finished. Oh, but this is sport!"

The White Rocking Horse and the Elephant, who wore roller skates, were close together, making their way as fast as they could toward the elevators. This was the half-way mark of the race. The two animals must turn around and come back to the toy counter before it would be known which was the faster. Just now they seemed to be even.

On and on they raced, faster and faster. If you had been there you would have enjoyed it, I am sure. But of course that was not allowed. If you had so much as peeped, even with one eye, the toys would instantly have become as motionless as the pictures in your spelling book.

Back and forth rocked the White Horse. Rumble and roll went the Elephant on his skates. They were close to the elevators in about three minutes after they had started from the crack mark.

"Now they are going to turn around," whispered the Celluloid Doll, as she leaned over the edge of the counter.

"Oh, look!" suddenly called the Monkey on a Stick. "Now the White
Rocking Horse will win the race!"

As he spoke there came a loud clattering sound down near the elevators—the halfway mark of the race. All the toys strained their necks to look, and they saw that one of the roller skates had come off the Elephant. He had turned too quickly, and had lost a skate.

"Never mind! Go on! Go on!" cried the Elephant, who was quite a sporting chap in his own way. "Go on with the race! I can beat you on three skates, Mr. Horse!"

"Ho! Ho! We'll see about that!" whinnied the rocking chap, as he made the turn and started back.

The two toys were going along as fast as they could, the rumble of the rockers on the White Horse mingling with the roll of the skates on the Elephant, when, all of a sudden, a brighter light shone in the toy department, the tread of footsteps was heard, and the Calico Clown had just time to shout:

"The watchman! To your places, every one!"

And instantly the toys were as motionless and quiet as mice. The Elephant, even on three skates, had been going so fast that he rolled behind a big pillar all covered with red and green tissue paper, with which the toy section was decorated. And the White Rocking Horse stayed just where he was when the Clown called out. Up among the toy counters and shelves came a big man carrying a lantern. He was the store watchman, and he went about in the different departments each night to see that all was well.

"What's this?" exclaimed the watchman, as he noticed the White Rocking Horse near the elevators. "This toy is out of place! He belongs over near the counter. Some clerk or customer must have left him here when the store closed last night. I'll take him back," and, picking up the White Rocking Horse, the watchman carried the toy back to where it belonged. And the Horse did not dare give even the smallest kick. He dared not show that he had been alive and in a race.

The watchman walked back toward the elevator, and saw the skate that had come off the Elephant's foot. He did not see the Elephant who was hidden behind the pillar.

"Well, I do declare!" exclaimed the watchman. "The clerks here are getting very careless! This roller skate belongs over in the sporting section. I'll take it there."

He picked it up and walked away. When he was gone, and the light of his lantern no longer gleamed, the Calico Clown slowly raised his head.

"Now you can go on with the race," he said.

"No, the race is spoiled for to-night," answered the Horse. "It will soon be daylight, and the clerks and shoppers will be coming in."

"Yes, and I would have to go to the other part of the store to get back my roller skate," said the Elephant. "I find I cannot get along on three. We'll have the race to-morrow night, Mr. Horse."

"That will suit me very well," said the proud, brave steed.

"And now we had all better get quiet," said the Monkey on a Stick. "I can see the sun peeping up in the east. Daylight is coming, and we dare no longer move about and talk. We have had some fun, but now we must get ready to be looked at by the shoppers. Quiet, everybody!"

And, as he spoke, the light suddenly grew stronger in the toy department, the clerks presently began coming in, and soon, when the sun was a little higher in the sky, the shoppers began arriving.

The White Rocking Horse, proud and stiff, stood near the counter. How his red saddle, of real leather, glistened in the light! How fluffy were his mane and tail!

Suddenly there came marching down the aisle of the store a boy whose feet made a great deal of noise, and who had a loud voice.

"Here's the Rocking Horse I want!" he cried. "I'm going to have this one!" And in an instant he had leaped on the back of the White Horse, banging his heels on the painted sides and yanking on the leather reins.

"Gid-dap! Gid-dap!" cried the rude boy, and he began kicking the White
Rocking Horse in the ribs.

CHAPTER III

A NICE MAN

"Dear me!" thought the White Rocking Horse to himself, as he felt the boy banging hard, leather heels into his side. "This is quite dreadful! I hope I am not sold to this boy! He would be a very unpleasant master to have, I am sure!"

Just because the White Rocking Horse and the other toys could not talk and move about when human eyes were watching them, did not stop them from thinking things to themselves, or from having feelings. And you may be very sure the White Rocking Horse felt that his feelings were very much hurt when the boy banged his heels so hard into the sides of the steed.

"I certainly hope I am not going to belong to this boy," thought the White Rocking Horse, and he looked toward the toy counter. He saw the Calico Clown glancing sadly at him, and he noticed the Monkey on a Stick making funny faces at the boy.

"I wish I could make that boy come over here and look at me," thought the Monkey. "Then he would let my friend, the White Rocking Horse, alone."

But the rude boy seemed to like being in the red leather saddle on the back of the Rocking Horse.

"Grid-dap! Go 'long there!" cried the boy, and again he clapped his heels against the wooden sides of the Horse, chipping off bits of paint. With his hands the boy yanked on the reins until he nearly pulled them off the head of the White Rocking Horse.

A young lady clerk, who worked in the toy department, came along just then.

"Please do not be so rough on the Horse, little boy," she said in a gentle voice.

"I'm going to have this Horse!" shouted the rude boy, as he rocked to and fro. "I'm going to make my mother buy him for me for Christmas. Go 'long! Gid-dap!"

"Oh, I never could stand belonging to this boy!" thought the poor White Rocking Horse. "I should want to run away!"

While the unpleasant boy was still in the saddle, swaying to and fro and banging his heels, a lady came walking down the aisle of the toy department.

"Here's the Horse I want!" the boy cried to her. "He's a dandy! He has real hair in his tail and mane, and the saddle is real leather! Buy me this Horse!"

"No, Reginald, I cannot buy you this Horse," said the lady. "It costs too much, and you have a rocking horse at home now."

"Yes, but that one has no ears, his leg is broken, and he has no saddle or bridle," cried the boy. "I want this horse!"

"Your horse was as good as this one when it was new," said the boy's mother. "If you had taken care of it, it would be a good horse yet."

"Well, I couldn't help it 'cause his ears pulled off! I wanted him to stop rocking and he wouldn't!" grumbled the rude boy. "I had to pull his ears!"

"Gracious! Think of pulling off the ears of a rocking horse because he wouldn't stay quiet!" said the Bold Tin Soldier to himself. "I hope our White Horse doesn't get this boy for a master."

"I want this Horse! I want this one!" cried the boy, again banging his heels on the side of the toy.

"No, Reginald, you cannot have it," said his mother,

"Then I want this Calico Clown!" the boy exclaimed, jumping off the horse so quickly that the toy animal would have been knocked over, only the young lady clerk caught it and held it upright.

The boy caught the Clown up in his hands, and began punching the toy in the chest to make the cymbals bang together.

"Dear me, what a dreadful chap this boy is!" thought the Calico Clown.
"So rough!"

As for the White Rocking Horse, he began to feel better as soon as the boy was out of the saddle. True, his wooden sides were somewhat dented, but the young lady clerk said to her friend at the doll counter:

"I'll get a little oil and rub the spots out. They won't show, and the Horse will be as good as ever. It's a shame such boys are allowed in the toy department."

"Buy me this Calico Clown!" cried the boy, who was punching the gaily dressed toy, and making the cymbals clang. "I want this, if I can't have the Rocking Horse!"

"No, you can't have anything until Christmas," said his mother. "Put it back, Reginald!"

The boy frowned and tossed the Calico Clown back on the counter so hard one of the cymbals struck the Candy Rabbit and chipped a little piece of sugar off one ear.

And all the toys were glad when the boy's mother finally took him away.

"I must get you a pair of shoes, Reginald," she said.

"I hope she gets him a pair that pinches his toes!" thought the Bold Tin Soldier. "Such boys should be taught not to break toys, and they never, never should be allowed to pull the ears off a rocking horse."

And if the White Rocking Horse could have spoken, he would have said the same thing, I am sure.

Other boys came in to try the White Rocking Horse, and they were all good boys. They took their place in the red saddle very quietly, and did not bang with their heels. Nor did they yank and seesaw on the reins that were fastened on the head of the Rocking Horse.

"I would rather belong to two, or even three, of these good, kind boys, than to that one rude chap," said the White Rocking Horse to himself, as he swayed backward and forward on the floor in the toy department. He and the Lamb on Wheels were too large to be set on the counter with the Calico Clown, the Monkey on a Stick, the Candy Rabbit and the Bold Tin Soldier and other smaller toys.

Slowly the day passed, and night was again coming on. Lights began to glow, for the days were short and evening came quickly—even before the store was closed.

"I wonder if the Rocking Horse and the Elephant will finish their race tonight?" thought the Bold Tin Soldier, as he felt himself being taken out of his box to be looked at by a lady who was doing her Christmas shopping.

It was almost closing time in the store when the White Rocking Horse, who felt much better since his sides had been rubbed with oil, heard a gentleman's voice speaking near him.

"This is about what I want for Dick's Christmas," said the man to the young lady clerk. "Is this a good Rocking Horse?"

"The best in the store; yes, sir," was the answer. "The tail and mane are real hair, and the saddle and bridle are real leather. The rockers, too, are nice and smooth, so the Horse will go fast."

"Well, I don't want it to go too fast," said the man, smiling down at the White Rocking Horse as he patted its neck, "My son Dick is too small to ride even a rocking horse very fast. I think, though, that I will have Santa Claus bring him this one. And, as it is so near Christmas, and as you are so very busy, if you will have this wrapped up for me, I will take it home in my auto. I will help Santa Claus that much."

"I'm sure he'll be glad to have you help him," replied the young lady, with a smile. "And I hope Dick will like this Horse. I am glad our Horse is going to a boy who will be kind to him."

"Oh, Dick takes good care of his toys," said the man.

"Well, thank goodness for that!" thought the White Rocking Horse. "Now like the Sawdust Doll, my adventures are going to start."

And, if you will turn to the next chapter, you may read what happened.

CHAPTER IV

THE SURPRISE

Through all this talk between the young lady of the store and the father who was buying something for his son's Christmas, to help busy Santa Claus, the White Rocking Horse never said a word. But he was doing as much thinking as a wooden horse ever did; I am sure of that.

"I'll get some big sheets of paper and wrap the horse up for you," said the young lady clerk to the man. "Are you sure you can get him in your auto?"

"Oh, yes," the man answered. "I have plenty of room. There will be no one in the car but the horse and myself. We shall have a nice ride together. It will seem rather funny to be giving a horse a ride in an automobile. I have often seen a horse pull a broken or stalled automobile along the street, but I never saw a horse in an auto before," he said.

"And I never did, either," replied the young lady, with a laugh, as she went to get the wrapping paper. "But then you know," she added, "this is not a regular horse."

"No, he is a rocking chap," said the man. Then he turned to another part of the toy department.

And as the young lady clerk was gone to get the paper and as the man was around the corner, over near the table where the checkers and dominoes were arranged in piles, the toys about which I have been telling you were left to themselves for a moment. And, of course, as there was no one to see them, they could move about and talk, if they wished. And they certainly did.

"Where do you suppose you are going?" asked the Calico Clown of the

White Rocking Horse.

"I haven't the least idea," was the answer. "But I know one thing: I am very sorry to leave you, my friends. We have had some jolly times together. Only think—last night the Elephant and I were having a friendly race!"

"Yes, and I wish I could have seen the finish of it," said the Bold Tin Soldier. "I am sure you would have won. A Rocking Horse is always faster than an Elephant."

"I am not so sure about that," said the Monkey on a Stick. "I believe the Elephant would have beaten."

"Well, we can't have the race now, that's sure," neighed the Horse. "I shall soon be leaving you."

"Maybe I could race with the Elephant," suggested the woolly Lamb. "I have wheels on, and if the Elephant wears his roller skates that will make us both even. We could have the race to-night, perhaps."

"Well, I hope you have jolly times when I am gone," said the White Rocking Horse. "Try to amuse yourselves."

"We will," answered the Calico Clown. "But perhaps you will come back to see us, as the Sawdust Doll once did."

"I'm afraid not," neighed the Horse. "You see, the Sawdust Doll came back because the little girl, whose mother bought the toy, carried the Doll in her arms. But I am too big to be carried in a boy's arms."

"Yes, that is so," agreed the Bold Tin Soldier. "Horses have to travel along by themselves, or else ride in autos. But perhaps, my dear friend, you may get a chance to gallop back here to see us some night."

"I should like to," the White Rocking Horse said; "but I don't see how it can be done. Some one would be sure to be looking."

"Hush! Quiet, everybody!" whispered the Calico Clown. "The man is coming back!"

And back he came, having finished looking at the checkers and dominoes. The young lady clerk also returned, with some large sheets of wrapping paper and a ball of string.

The toys could talk among themselves no longer, but of course they could still think, and each one who was to be left behind thought how lonesome it would be with the White Rocking Horse gone.

As for that wonderful chap, he was soon covered from the sight of his friends in the wrappings of paper. One sheet was put over his head, so he could see nothing more. Then his body and legs were wrapped in other papers, and the red saddle and bridle of real leather were covered up, as were the mane and tail of real hair.

"There, I think he will ride very nicely in my auto now," said the man, as he paid the clerk for the White Rocking Horse. Then the man carried the Horse down in the elevator.

At first it made the White Rocking Horse a little dizzy to be carried down in the elevator. He had not ridden in one for a long time—not since he was first brought to the big store from the Land of the North Pole, where he had been made in the work-shop of Santa Claus. Then the White Rocking Horse had been carried up to the toy department in a big freight elevator, with many others like himself. But that freight elevator went more slowly than the passenger one in which the man now carried down his boy's Christmas present, thus helping St. Nicholas, who was to be very busy that year.

As the man went outside the store with his bundle the White Rocking Horse felt a cold chill run over him. He was so used to the warm store that he had forgotten the cold weather outside. It was snowing, too, and one or two white flakes sifted in through cracks of the wrapping paper, and fell on the Horse.

"Well, this is certainly a strange adventure," thought the White Horse; "being carried along this way, out into a storm. I wonder what will happen next?"

And the next he knew he was put in the back of an automobile and away he rode, faster than he ever could have traveled by himself—

faster even than he had gone while racing with the Elephant on roller skates.

The ride in the automobile through the snow made the White Rocking Horse rather sleepy, so he really did not know much about what happened on his trip through the storm. All he remembered was that he went quite fast and at last the car stopped.

Then he felt himself being lifted out of the automobile, and he heard voices.

"Is Dick out of the way?" the man asked.

"Yes, he and Dorothy are up in the playroom," was the answer in a lady's voice. "You can carry the Horse right up to the attic. He can stay there until Santa Claus is ready to put him under the Christmas tree."

"All right," said the man. "As long as Dick and Dorothy are out of the way I'll bring the Horse in. I don't want them to see it until Christmas."

"Dorothy! Dorothy!" thought the Horse to himself. "Where have I heard that name before? I guess some little girl who was called that must have come to the toy department at one time or another. Well, now to see what happens next!"

He felt himself being carried along. Dimly he saw lights, and he felt that he was in a warm place—as warm as the store had been. Then, suddenly, the wrapping papers were taken off him.

"Oh, what a beautiful Rocking Horse!" exclaimed the lady. "I am sure Dick will be pleased. It's the same one I saw in the store. I am glad you got that one!"

Now the White Rocking Horse was still rather dazed and still rather sleepy from his ride in the cold. Or else perhaps he would have been prepared for the surprise in store for him. Dimly he seemed to remember having heard that lady's voice before, and dimly he recalled having seen her before.

Then, when his wrapping papers had been taken off, he was set down on the floor near a warm chimney in rather a bare and cheerless attic, and left to himself in the darkness.

But the White Rocking Horse could see in the dark. And when he knew that no human eyes were watching him he spoke, in the make-believe language of toy land.

"Is any one here—any toy to whom I can talk, and with whom I can have a little fun?" asked the White Horse out loud.

There was no answer for a moment, and then a voice said:

"You can talk to me, if you like, but it has been many years since I have had any fun. I am old and broken and covered with dust."

"Who are you?" asked the White Horse.

"I am an old Jumping Jack," was the answer. "Here I am, over by the chimney."

"Oh, now I see you!" said the Horse. "But what is the matter? Are you so very old?"

"Oh, yes, I am almost five Christmases old," was the answer. "My two legs are broken, and one of my arms, and the spring by which I used to jump is all worn out. So, as I am no longer of any use in this world, I am in the Attic Home. That is the last resting place of broken toys, you know."

"I have heard of it," said the Rocking Horse rather sadly. "I hope I am not kept here."

"Indeed you will not be," said the old Jumping Jack. "You are new, and are going to enjoy your first Christmas! Ah, how well I remember that! But there is no use worrying. I had some good times, I once made a little boy happy, and now I am content to stay here in the dust and darkness. I shall be glad to know that you are going to have a jolly time."

"Thank you," said the White Rocking Horse.

Then he and the old Jumping Jack talked together for some hours in the attic. All the next day they were together, and the White Rocking Horse told how he had once lived in a big department store, and how he had been given a ride in an automobile. And the Jumping Jack told his story, how he used to leap about and cut funny capers.

The next night, after dark, a light was seen gleaming in the attic. The White Rocking Horse and the Jumping Jack had just begun to talk together, and the Horse was showing his friend how fast he could rock, when they had to stop, because the man came up. The lady was with him.

"Dick and Dorothy are asleep now," said the lady. "We can take the Rocking Horse down, and leave him for Santa Claus to put under the big Christmas tree."

"Yes, we can do that," the man said. "And here is an old Jumping Jack.
It is broken, but the paint on it is still gay. I'll dust it off and take it down for the Christmas tree. It will make it look more jolly."
And to his own great surprise the Jack was taken down with the White
Rocking Horse.

As for the Rocking Horse, so many things happened at once that he hardly knew where one began and the other left off. He saw some gleaming lights and red, blue, green and golden-yellow balls that seemed brighter than the sun. He saw a big, green tree. He saw many toys scattered under it. And one, in particular, made him open his eyes in wonder.

For there, sitting on the carpet near him, was the Sawdust Doll! The very-same Sawdust Doll who had lived in the toy store with him!

CHAPTER V

A NIGHT RIDE

The White Rocking Horse wanted to gallop across the room and back, because he felt so happy at seeing the Sawdust Doll again. As for the Sawdust Doll, she wanted to stand up and clap her hands, as the Calico Clown used to clap his cymbals together. But neither of the toys dared do anything, because, in the same room with them, were the father and mother of Dick and Dorothy. And the toys, as I told you, never moved or spoke when any one was near them.

"The old Jumping Jack looks well on the Christmas tree," said the lady, as she smoothed out the dress of the Sawdust Doll.

"Yes, I'm glad we brought him down out of the attic, poor fellow," replied the man, as he rocked the Horse slowly to and fro, to make sure he was in a good place. "I wonder if these toys ever know or care what joy they give to the children?" he asked.

"Oh, I think they do," said Dorothy's mother. "Do you know," she went on with a little laugh, "sometimes I think the toys are really alive, and can talk among themselves, and do things."

"What nonsense!" laughed the man. "Do you think this Rocking Horse can come to life?" and he patted our toy friend.

"Well, maybe not exactly come to life," answered his wife. "But I am sure they must have good times when we aren't looking. See that Sawdust Doll! Why, I really think she is looking at the

Rocking Horse as if she knew him! And you know they did come from the same store."

"Well, I think everything is ready now for Santa Claus," said the man. "We will leave the rest of the tree to him. It will soon be Christmas morning. Let us go out and leave the toys to themselves. Perhaps they will really have a good time, as you think."

"I am sure they will," the lady said, laughing softly.

Then the door was shut and of course you can guess what happened when no human eyes were there to watch the White Rocking Horse and Sawdust Doll.

The Doll was the first to speak.

"Oh, how glad I am to see you!" she said, as she stood up on her sawdust-stuffed legs and looked at the Horse high above her head. "You can't imagine how glad I am!"

"And I am glad to see you," neighed the Horse. "I never dreamed I should be brought to the house where you were. Tell me, are you to be a Christmas present, too?"

"No, I was bought for Dorothy's birthday," was the answer. "Don't you remember? I left the store some weeks ago. But Dorothy wanted me put under the Christmas tree with the other presents Santa Claus is to bring to her and Dick. But you are a Christmas present, I know."

"Yes, I am," said the White Rocking Horse. "Real jolly, I call it! I never saw a Christmas tree before."

"You haven't really seen this one yet," went on the Sawdust Doll. "Has he, Jumping Jack?" she asked.

"Indeed I should say not," was the reply. "It has not been lighted as yet. I well remember the first Christmas tree I was put on. I was a gay, jumping chap then. My spring wasn't broken. But I am not going to talk about that. This is no time for sadness. Only, when the tree is lighted to-morrow night, Rocking Horse, you will see something very pretty. Will he not, Sawdust Doll?"

"He certainly will! And now, please tell me about my friends in the store," she begged. "How are the Bold Tin Soldier and the Calico Clown?"

"Each sent you his love," said the White Horse. "And the Candy Rabbit, the Lamb on Wheels and the Monkey on a Stick—each and every one wanted to be remembered to you."

"That was very kind of them, I'm sure," said the Sawdust Doll. "But tell me—have you had any fun since I left?"

"Oh, a little," was the answer. "Only last night the Elephant, who borrowed some roller skates, started to race with me," said the Rocking Horse. "We got as far as the elevators, but one of his skates came off. We started back and then the watchman came in and spoiled the fun."

"What a shame!" cried the Sawdust Doll. "I wish I had been there to see. But I am so glad you have come to live here."

"Is it a nice place?" asked the Horse.

"Oh, the very nicest!" exclaimed the Sawdust Doll. "Dorothy is such a kind mistress to me. And you will find her brother Dick a kind master, too. I suppose you are going to belong to him."

"Well, I haven't really heard much about it," said the Horse. "A number of boys came into the store and tried to ride me. One gave me some hard kicks in my side—so hard that I was afraid all my paint would come off. But a girl in the store oiled me, and I am all right again. I think I remember Dick."

"Yes, he was in the store once, when. Dorothy's mother brought her little girl in to look at dolls, and I was the one the mother picked out because I had such brown eyes."

"*Nice* brown eyes, I think she said," cried the Rocking Horse.

"Well, of course it would not do for me to say that," said the Sawdust Doll, smiling. "At any rate, here we two are, together, and in a happy home, and I am glad of it."

"So am I," the Rocking Horse said.

[Illustration: White Rocking Horse is Glad to See Sawdust Doll Again.]

"And I am, too," came from the Jumping Jack. "If it had not been for you, my rocking friend," he went on, "I might be still dust-covered and in the attic." So the toys under the Christmas tree talked among themselves and even moved about a little, but not too much, for they could not tell at what moment some one might come in.

And in the night Christmas came. The toys under the tree knew it just as well as if they had been real persons. They knew Santa Claus a great deal better than most real persons, too, having been made in the North Pole shop of St. Nicholas.

"Well, you will soon have Dick riding on your back," said the Sawdust Doll to the Rocking Horse as, together, they waited beneath the green tree. "I can see the morning light coming over the hills. And I heard Dorothy and Dick saying yesterday that they were going to get up, even before the sun, to see what Santa Claus had brought them."

"He certainly brought them a fine lot of presents," remarked the Jumping Jack, in a sort of rusty, squeaking voice. "I hope—"

"Hush! Here they come, now!" whispered the Sawdust Doll.

The door opened. In rushed two happy, laughing, shouting children.

"Merry Christmas!" cried Dorothy.

"Merry Christmas!" echoed Dick.

"Oh, here is the set of dishes I wanted!" Dorothy exclaimed.

"And here is my White Rocking Horse!" shouted Dick. "Oh, it's just the very one I hoped I'd get! Oh, what a dandy!"

With a leap he was up on the red saddle and grasping the red reins in his hands.

"Gid-dap!" cried the boy, and he beat a tattoo on the sides of the horse with his feet. But as Dick had on soft slippers, he did not hurt the White Rocking Horse in the least, nor did he chip off any paint. "Here I go! Here I go!" shouted Dick. "Oh, what a fine horse!"

"He's lovely, Dick," said his sister.

"Merry Christmas, children!" said Mother, as she came in to see the Christmas tree.

"Merry Christmas!" they answered. "See what you have, Mother!"

And there were presents for her and for Daddy also, under the tree. And Daddy came downstairs, rubbing his eyes and saying:

"Merry Christmas!"

The White Rocking Horse felt very happy and so did the Sawdust Doll, and even the Jumping Jack was as jolly as the rest.

"You may have a ride on my horse if you want to, Dorothy," said Dick, as he slowly brought his steed to a stop.

"Thank you," answered his sister. "And when I have a play party with my new Christmas dishes you may come and have some cake."

And so Christmas came and brought happiness with it to Dick and Dorothy and also to the White Rocking Horse and the Sawdust Doll. For the toys were in a fine house and had a kind master and mistress. And that means more than you think to toys.

I cannot begin to tell you all that happened this Christmas Day. Boy and girl playmates of Dorothy and Dick came over to see what Santa Claus had brought their friends, and the visitors showed their own presents. Among the callers were Mirabell and Arnold, the boy and girl who lived next door.

"Oh, what nice things you have!" said Mirabell. "I got nice presents, too. I wanted a Lamb on Wheels, such as I once saw in the store, but I have so many things I don't exactly need that now. Maybe I'll get one later on."

"And I wanted a Bold Tin Soldier," said Arnold, her brother. "But I have a pop gun and a drum, and I'll wait until my birthday for the soldier."

The children had jolly Christmas fun, and at night the tree was lighted.

"Oh, what a beautiful sight!" said the White Rocking Horse to the Sawdust Doll, when they were alone in the room for a moment and could talk without being overheard.

"I told you that you'd see something wonderful," said the old Jumping
Jack.

"You were right," said the Rocking Horse. "It is beautiful!"

The fun of Christmas night was as jolly as that during the day, but at last Mother said:

"Come now, children, it is time to go to sleep. You may play with your White Rocking Horse to-morrow, Dick. And you may have a play party for your Sawdust Doll, Dorothy."

And, very happy indeed, brother and sister went to bed.

It became very still and quiet and dark in the house. It was like the hour in the department store when there is no one to see the toys.

"Now I can move about," said the White Rocking Horse, who had been taken up to Dick's room. "I wish I could see the Sawdust Doll and have a talk with her."

"She is in Dorothy's room," said an old Driver, who had once sat on a tin express wagon. "Dorothy always takes her doll to bed with her."

"Then I think I'll go in and see my friend," said the Horse. "I can gallop softly down the hall and into Dorothy's room. As long as no one sees me I am allowed to move about."

"Yes, go ahead," said the Driver. "I'd go with you if I still had my wagon. Go and see the Sawdust Doll."

So rocking softly over the thick carpet, and making no noise, the White Horse made his way out of Dick's room, down the hall, and straight to where Dorothy was sleeping with the Sawdust Doll on the pillow beside her.

CHAPTER VI

THE BROKEN LEG

The White Rocking Horse stopped in the hall outside of Dorothy's room. The door was open, and in the dim glow of a night-light the Horse could see the Sawdust Doll on the bed.

"Hi there! Hist! Come on out here and have a talk!" called the Rocking

Horse.

"What's that? Who is calling me?" asked the Sawdust Doll, for she had fallen asleep, being rather tired from having had so much Christmas fun that day.

"I am calling you," answered the White Rocking Horse. "Come on out into the hall. I don't want to come in, for fear some one might come along. And it would never do to let it be known that we toys can move and talk when no one sees us."

"Indeed, no; never!" exclaimed the Sawdust Doll. "Wait a minute and I'll come out to you. As you say, it would not do to be caught. I'll slip down and come out."

The White Rocking Horse waited in the hall. Soon he heard a little thud on the carpet. That was the Sawdust Doll sliding down out of Dorothy's bed to the floor. A moment later she stood beside the Rocking Horse in the hall.

"I hope you won't take cold," said the Horse softly. "It is breezy in this hall."

"Oh, no, I have a nice little warm shawl Dorothy made for me," answered the Sawdust Doll. "Thank you for thinking of me, though."

"Well, you see I want to be able to take a good report of you back to your friends in the toy store," neighed the Horse.

"Do you think you will ever get back there again?" the Doll asked, as she snuggled up in a corner, wrapping the shawl around her.

"I don't know," the Horse replied. "Of course I could rock back to the store if no one saw me, but it is a long way, and if I went through the streets I'd almost certainly be seen."

"I think so, too," said the Doll. "I'm afraid we shall just have to stay here together the rest of our lives."

"Well, I like it in this house since you are here," said the Horse. "And who knows, perhaps some of the other toys may join us here on some future Christmas or birthday."

"Wouldn't that be fine!" exclaimed the Doll, clapping her hands. "I'd dearly love to see the Bold Tin Soldier again, and the Calico Clown, the Lamb on Wheels, the Candy Rabbit and the Monkey on a Stick."

"I'd like to finish the race with the Elephant on his roller skates," said the Horse, laughing softly. "But I don't suppose I ever shall. He did look so funny when one skate came off!"

"I wish I had been there to see," said the Sawdust Doll. "Now tell me all that happened in the store after I left."

So the Horse told of the different happenings, how sometimes rough boys ran in and jumped on his back, and how one unpleasant chap punched the Calico Clown so hard that the cymbals were nearly broken, and how the Candy Rabbit had a bit of sugar chipped from one ear.

"Dear me! How exciting!" cried the Sawdust Doll.

"And now tell me about yourself," urged the White Rocking Horse. "Have you had any adventures??"

"Oh, I should say I had! Yes, indeed!" was the answer. "Did I tell you about the time Dick ran over me with the rocking chair, pretending it was a Horse like you? My sawdust ran out of a hole in my side, and I fainted!"

"No! Really? Did you?"

"Indeed I did. It was the strangest feeling!"

"But I should think, if all your sawdust ran out—and, really, how terrible that must have been—you wouldn't be here any more," said the Horse.

"Oh, it didn't *all* run out!" the Doll answered. "Dorothy's father hurried to the carpenter shop and got more sawdust, and Dorothy's mother sewed it, up in me so I was all right again."

"I'm glad of that," remarked the White Rocking Horse.

"So am I," said the Doll. "But do you know, since then, I have not been quite the same."

"In what way?" asked the White Rocking Horse.

"Well, I seem to have a little indigestion," went on the Sawdust Doll.
"I think the carpenter shop sawdust they stuffed into me was not the same kind that was put in me when I was made in the North Pole shop of Santa Claus."

"Very likely not," agreed the Horse. "All sawdust is not alike. But still you are looking rather well."

"I am glad you think so," remarked the Doll. "But now let us talk of something pleasant. Tell me, again, about the race you had with the Elephant on his roller skates."

So the White Horse did, but as you know as much of that funny race   as
I do, there is no need of putting it in here again.

So the two friends talked together in the hall until, all of a sudden, the Doll exclaimed:

"Oh, it is getting daylight! We must go back to our places—you to
Dick's room and I to Dorothy's. Quick!"

The White Rocking Horse galloped back down the hall, and the Doll made her way into the room of the little girl whose birthday present she was.

Now whether the carpenter shop sawdust was not the right kind to enable the Doll to move quickly enough, and whether the oil the clerk had rubbed on the side of the Horse made him a bit slow and slippery, I cannot say. Anyhow, daylight suddenly broke just as the Doll reached the side of Dorothy's bed, and before she had time to climb up into it by taking hold of the blankets.

As for the Horse, he was only half way inside Dick's room when the sun came up and awakened both children. And of course, their eyes being open, Dorothy looking at her Doll and Dick at his Horse, neither toy dared move.

"Oh! Oh!" cried Dick, when he saw that his White Rocking Horse was on the other side of the room from where he had left it when he went to sleep the night before. "Oh! Oh! Some one had my Horse!"

"What makes you think so?" asked his father, coming in to see what Dick was shouting about.

"Because he's moved," the little boy answered. "My Rocking Horse has moved!"

"I guess the wind blew him," said Daddy. "The wind from your open window blew on the horse, made him rock to and fro, and he moved in that way."

But Dick shook his head.

"Either my Horse moved by himself in the night when I was asleep," he said, "or else somebody was riding him."

And when Dorothy awakened and saw her Doll lying on the carpet just under the edge of the bed, the little girl cried out, as Dick had done:

"Oh! Oh! Oh!"

"What's the matter?" asked Mother, hurrying in.

"Somebody took my Doll out of bed, or else she got out herself in the night!" said Dorothy.

"She probably fell out," said Mother, with a laugh. "The Doll couldn't get out herself, and no one has been in your room."

But we know what happened, don't we?

One day, about a week after Christmas, there came a warm, sunny day.

"May I take my Rocking Horse out on the porch and ride him?" asked
Dick of his mother.

"Yes," she answered.

"And I'll take my Sawdust Doll out there, and maybe Mirabell and
Arnold will come over and we can have a play party," said Dorothy.

The children went out on the porch, and they could look over next door and see their two little friends.

"See how fast I can ride my horse!" called Dick to Arnold.

The boy got up on the back of the White Horse and rocked to and fro. And the Horse traveled across the porch, as a rocking chair sometimes travels across the room.

"Oh, he's a fine Horse!" cried Arnold, as he came over to play, bringing his toy train of cars with him. And Mirabell brought her wax doll. "Let me ride him, Dick, will you?"

After Dick and Arnold had taken turns riding on the White Horse, they left him on the edge of the porch to play with the toy train. Suddenly Carlo, the fuzzy dog that had once carried the Sawdust Doll out to his kennel, hiding her in the straw, ran around the corner of the house, barking loudly.

"Bow-wow! Bow-wow!" barked Carlo, and he ran straight for the White
Rocking Horse.

How it happened no one seemed to know, but Carlo upset the Horse, which tumbled down the porch steps with many a bang and bump.

"Dear me!" thought the Horse, "This is not a pleasant adventure at all! What is going to happen?"

"Bang! Bump! Crack!" sounded he rolled over and over down the steps.

"Oh, what a pain in my leg!" said White Rocking Horse to himself.

Dick ran over to his toy, and when he saw his White Horse lying on the sidewalk at the foot of the steps, the little boy cried:

"Oh, his leg is broken! Oh, the leg of my White Rocking Horse is broken! I can never ride him again!"

CHAPTER VII

IN THE TOY HOSPITAL

Dick made such a fuss out on the porch, crying, when he saw his toy lying at the foot of the steps, that the boy's mother hurried out to see what the trouble was.

"Dear me! Did you fall off?" asked Mother, as she saw the Horse lying on its side and Dick standing at the bottom of the porch steps near his toy. "Are you hurt, Sonny?"

"Oh, no, Mother. But my Horse is! My Christmas Horse is hurt."

"You can't hurt a wooden rocking horse," said Mother, as she went over to see what had happened.

"Oh, yes you can!" sobbed Dick, for he was so little a boy that he was not ashamed to cry. "My Horse's leg is broken! I can never ride him again! Oh, dear!"

Mother looked at the Horse lying on its side at the foot of the steps. If there had been no one there to look on, the Horse might have tried to get up, even with all his pain. But, as it was against the rules to move or say anything as long as human eyes were watching, the poor White Rocking Horse just had to lie there.

"Dear me, one of the legs really is broken," said Mother, as she set the Horse upright. And, being a wooden horse with rockers under him, such as some chairs have, the Horse could stand upright, even though one of his legs was cracked clear through.

"Yes, his leg is broken, and now I can never have a ride on him any more!" sobbed Dick. "Oh, dear!"

"Oh, it isn't as bad as all that," said Mother, with a kind smile as she patted her little boy's head. "I think we can have the broken leg mended. But how did it happen? Did you ride your Horse off the porch, Dick?"

"No, Mother," he answered. "I was playing with Arnold's train, and Carlo ran around the corner, barking, and he ran between my Horse's legs, I guess, and upset him. Oh, isn't it too bad?"

"Yes; but it might be worse," replied Mother. "If *your* leg had been broken, or Dorothy's or Mirabell's or Arnold's, it could not so easily be mended."

"Can you mend the broken leg of my White Rocking Horse?" asked Dick eagerly.

"I cannot mend it, myself," Mother answered. "But I will have Daddy take your Horse to the hospital."

"I was in the hospital once," put in Arnold, "and I had some bread and jelly."

"Will they give my Horse bread and jelly in the hospital?" asked Dick of Mother.

"Hardly that," she replied with a smile. "It is not the same kind of hospital. The one where I will have Daddy take your White Rocking Horse is a toy hospital, where all sorts of broken playthings are mended. There your Horse will be made as good as new."

"Oh, I shall be so glad if he is," said Dick.

And the White Horse himself, though he dared say nothing just then, thought how glad he would be to have his broken leg mended. Some of the splinters were sticking him, and though of course I do not mean to say that a wooden horse has the same pain with a broken leg as a boy or girl or a chicken or a rooster would have, still it is no fun.

Patrick, the gardener, came out and carried the broken-legged Rocking
Horse into the front hall.

"We'll let him stand there until Daddy comes home with the auto and can take him to the hospital," said Mother.

And then it was that the White Rocking Horse had a chance to speak to the Sawdust Doll. Dorothy laid her Doll on a chair in the hall to help Dick, Mirabell and Arnold bring the toy train inside, as it was getting too cold to play out on the porch.

"I'm sorry," murmured the Doll.

[Illustration: What Happened to You?" Asked White Rocking Horse.]

"Oh, ho!" exclaimed Dick's Daddy, when he came home and heard the story. "A Rocking Horse with a broken leg! Of course I'll take him to the toy hospital."

And, not waiting for his supper, lest the hospital be closed, Daddy wrapped the White Rocking Horse in a sheet, put him once more in the back of the automobile and started off.

A little later the White Rocking Horse found himself in the toy hospital. It was not such a place as you have seen if you have ever been in the buildings where sick people are made well. There were no beds and no doctors and no queer smells. Yes, wait a minute, there were queer smells of glue and paste, but the White Rocking Horse rather liked them.

Instead of a doctor there was a jolly-looking man, with a long apron, and a square, paper cap.

"Can you mend the broken leg of this Rocking Horse?" asked Dick's father. The hospital toy doctor looked at the White Rocking Horse.

"I shall have to put a new piece in his leg," he said. "It is badly splintered half way down."

"Will it be as strong as before, so my little boy can ride?" asked Daddy.

"It will be even stronger," answered the hospital toy doctor. "I will have him ready for you in a few days; perhaps tomorrow."

"And will the broken leg show?" asked Daddy.

"Hardly any," was the reply. "I will paint it over so you will never know it."

"Then the Horse will be almost as good as ever," said Daddy.

"Just as good," said the toy doctor, and the Horse felt much better when he heard this. His leg did not pain him so much.

The hospital toy doctor set the White Rocking Horse over in one corner near a work bench. Dick's Daddy, after a look around the hospital started back home in his automobile.

"We'll soon have you fixed, my fine fellow!" said the toy doctor, as he again took up his work of putting a new pair of eyes in a wax doll. "We'll make as good a Horse of you as before."

"I certainly am glad of that," thought the Horse to himself.

It soon became too dark for the toy doctor to see to work any longer, even though he lighted the gas. So he took off his long apron, laid aside his square, paper cap, locked up the place and went home.

And then the White Rocking Horse took a long breath.

"Now that I am alone I'll move about, as well as I can on three legs, and talk to some of the broken toys here," said the White Rocking Horse aloud. "Are you badly hurt?" he asked a Jack in the Box, who was on the work-bench near by.

"My spring is gone," was the answer. "I was brought here to have a new one put in."

"Well, I hope you will soon be mended," said the White Horse. "I wonder if any of my friends are here in this hospital? I say, toys!" he cried, "let's all talk together and—"

All at once a big white paper spread out on the bench began to move, and out from under it came a toy, at the sight of which the Horse exclaimed:

"Well, I do declare! Who would have thought to find you here? What happened to you? Dear me, what a surprise!"

CHAPTER VIII

HOME AGAIN

Many of the toys, which had been mended since having been brought to the hospital, stood up and looked at the White Rocking Horse as he called to them, and they wondered what had surprised him so.

"My goodness, that Horse is making a great deal of noise," said a large Wooden Soldier, one of whose legs was in splints. It had been broken in three places when the little boy, who owned the Soldier, had struck him with a drumstick.

"I should say that Horse was making a great deal of noise," agreed a Tin Poodle Dog, whose tail needed straightening. "What's it all about, Mr. Horse?" he barked.

"Excuse me, my toy friends, I did not mean to disturb you," said the White Rocking Horse kindly. "But I was so surprised to see an old friend of mine here that I just couldn't help calling out."

"Who is your friend?" asked a Double Humped Camel from a Noah's Ark.

"There he is," said the Horse, and he waved his tail toward the animal which had come out from under the big piece of white paper on the work bench of the toy hospital doctor.

All the other toys looked, and saw an Elephant. But the White Rocking
Horse did more than look. He cried out:

"To think of seeing you here, my Elephant friend! Why, the last time we were together was in the toy store!"

"Yes, and I was trying to race with you on roller skates," said the Elephant, with a laugh. "Wasn't it funny when my skate came off?"

The other toys stared in interest.

"Very funny," agreed the Horse. "We must tell our friends here about it. But I am sorry to see what has happened to you, Mr. Elephant!" went on the Horse. "Did you get broken this way when you fell off the roller skates, or anything like that? You certainly do look queer—not at all like yourself!"

"And I don't feel like myself," said the Elephant.

Well might he say that, for his trunk was broken off short, and you know, as well as I do, that an elephant without a trunk doesn't look at all like himself. He might just as well, or even better, have no tail, as far as looks go.

"What happened to you?" asked the Horse.

"Oh, I have had many adventures," replied the Elephant. "After you were taken away by the man in the automobile, I was sold to a lady and a little boy and taken to their home."

"Was it a nice place?" the Horse wanted to know.

"The place was all right," the Elephant answered. "But that little boy! Dear me! I don't just know what to say about him, he certainly did not treat me very nicely. Why, do you know," he went on, speaking in rather a funny voice on account of his trunk being broken off, "he never gave me a single peanut all the while I was with him!"

"No! Really? Was he as unkind as that?" asked the broken Jack in the
Box.

"But that wasn't the worst," continued the Elephant. "After the boy had dropped some bread and jam on me, he thought he'd wash me off in the bath room. He took me up to carry me there, but he dropped me on the hard, tile floor and—well, you see what happened to me. My trunk was broken off—broken off short!"

"What a sad accident!" exclaimed the Horse.

"You may well say so," returned the Elephant. "The little boy was sorry for me, I'll say that of him. He called his mother and she tried to fix me. She glued my trunk on, but she got it crooked and when I saw myself in the glass I was ashamed! I was glad none of the other toy animals could see me."

"What happened next?" asked the Horse, as the Elephant stopped to catch his breath. It rather made him out of breath to talk without his trunk.

"Well, after the boy's mother glued my trunk on he played with me for a while, but he dropped me again, and my trunk broke off again in the same place. After that the boy's father said I had better come to the hospital. So here I am."

"But where is your trunk?" asked the Horse.

"Back under that piece of paper where I was sleeping," the big animal answered. "It is to be fastened on me properly tomorrow. The toy hospital doctor first washed the jam off me. I was made clean again, and I was glad of that. Then, to keep the dust off me, he put me under that paper. But when I heard you speaking, White Rocking Horse, I just had to come out, trunk or no trunk."

"I'm glad you did," said the White Rocking Horse. "Really, when I look at you again, I get rather used to seeing you without your trunk, though at first I hardly knew you. Do you suffer much now?"

"Not as much as I did," was the answer. "But I shall be all right after to-morrow, when my trunk is to be put back on. Then I suppose I'll go back to that boy's house."

"I hope he treats you better," said the White Horse.

"I think he will," replied the Elephant. "When his father took me away he said the boy could not have me back after I was mended until he knew how to handle his toys. So I have hopes of being better off with my mended trunk than before."

"Let us all hope so," sighed the Tin Poodle Dog. "It's queer how cruel some children are to us. They think, because we are toys, we have no feelings."

"Yes, that is so," said the White Horse. "But Dick, the boy who owns me, is very kind. It was an accident that my leg was broken. Carlo, a poodle dog something like you, my tin friend, only real, ran too close to me and knocked me down the steps," said the Horse to the Tin Poodle Dog.

"Oh, so you are injured, too, are you?" asked the Elephant. "I have been talking so much about myself, Mr. Horse, that I never thought to ask what your trouble was. Will you kindly pardon me?"

"Certainly," neighed the Horse, politely. "And now, as we are here by ourselves, and no one can see us, suppose we have a little fun-that is, as much fun as we can, broken and twisted as we are."

"Hurray! That's it! Let's have some fun!" cried the Tin Poodle Dog, with a funny little bark.

So the Elephant with the broken trunk told about his queer race on roller skates, the Horse spoke of the Christmas tree, and the other animals related their adventures. They had a good time together until morning came. Then, when it was time for the toy hospital doctor to come to his shop, the Elephant got back under the paper that was to keep him clean until he was mended, the Horse slowly hobbled back to his place, the Tin Poodle Dog leaned up against the broken Jack in the Box, and all the toys became as quiet as though they had never spoken or moved about.

"Hum, lots of work for me to-day!" said the toy hospital doctor, as he put on his apron and his square, paper cap. "I must mend the broken leg of that Rocking Horse as soon as I fix the Elephant's trunk."

Then the toy doctor took the Elephant from under the paper and, after blowing off a little dust, began work. He made a new piece of trunk out of wood and cloth, and painted it until it looked just like part of the Elephant. Then the two pieces were fastened together with wooden pins, and also some glue.

"There! Now you are stronger than you were before," said the toy hospital doctor, putting the Elephant on a shelf. "And now for the broken leg of the Rocking Horse. Dear me, that is quite a bad break," said the toy doctor. "I think I shall have to make him a whole new wooden leg."

The White Rocking Horse felt glad when he heard this. For he was rather a proud chap, and when he had seen part of the Elephant's old trunk put back on that animal, the Horse thought of how he would look with part of his old broken leg glued fast.

"I had much rather have a whole new leg," he said to himself.

And that is exactly what he had. Out of a piece of wood the toy doctor made a new leg for the Rocking Horse. He took off the old, splintered one, that had been broken in the fall off the porch. Then the new leg was put in place.

"There! When it's painted no one will ever know one of his legs was broken," said the toy doctor.

The new leg was smoothed with sandpaper, and then painted just the color of the other legs.

"I'm glad he painted my new leg," thought the Horse. "I would look very funny with three white legs and one brown or red one. Yes, this toy doctor is a very smart man. I feel quite myself now."

The toy hospital doctor was busy in his shop all day, mending things that children break in their play, and toward evening Dick's father came in.

"Is my boy's White Rocking Horse mended?" the man asked.

"Yes, all ready for you," answered the toy doctor. "I finished him sooner than I expected to. The paint is hardly dry, but it will be by morning. I made him a new leg."

"That's good!" exclaimed the man. "My little boy wants to ride his Rocking Horse. He misses him very much."

Back home went the White Rocking Horse. And when Dick saw him he clapped his hands and cried:

"Oh, how glad I am! May I take a ride?"

"If you are careful of the newly-painted leg," his father answered. "I'll lift you up into the saddle."

And when Dick sat in the red leather seat and pulled on the red reins and shouted to his Horse he was a very happy boy, and the White Rocking Horse felt glad also.

"Gid-dap!" called Dick. "Gid-dap, my Rocking Horse!" And the Horse galloped across the room.

All of a sudden Dorothy came running into the playroom where Dick sat on his Horse.

"Oh, Dick! Dick!" cried the little girl. "Come on down to the kitchen, quick! Carlo has something under a chair! Maybe it's a big mouse! Come and see!"

CHAPTER IX

TWO BAD MEN

Dick jumped off his Rocking Horse.

"What did you say Carlo had?" he asked his sister.

"I don't know," Dorothy answered. "But I was down in the kitchen, and Mary had just given me some bread and sugar, and I saw Carlo under a chair. He had something in his mouth and he was shaking it. And it was brown and fuzzy and maybe it's a mouse. You'd better come, 'cause Mary's standin' up on a chair and hollerin' awful loud. It's fun."

"Oh, I'll come!" cried Dick. "But where's Mother?"

"Oh, she's in the parlor with some ladies," answered the little girl. "I didn't tell her."

"That's right," said Dick, hurrying over to a closet in the playroom.

"What are you going to do?" asked Dorothy. "You'd better hurry if you want to help Carlo catch that mouse."

"I am hurrying," Dick said. "But I want to get my soldier cap and my pop gun."

"What for?" the little girl wanted to know.

"'Cause I'm going to make believe I'm a captain, and the mouse is an enemy, and I'm going to capture the enemy. Like in war."

Down to the kitchen the children hurried. They could hear their dog Carlo barking and growling, and they could hear Mary, the cook, laughing.

"She isn't very scared, I guess," said Dick.

"Well, she *was*, and she was up on a chair," declared Dorothy. "Come on, Dick!"

Together they hurried into the kitchen. Mary was no longer standing on a chair. Instead she was sitting down in one, laughing as hard as she could laugh.

Carlo was out in the middle of the floor, tossing up into the air something brown and fuzzy.

"Where's the mouse?" cried Dick. "I want to see if I can shoot it with my pop gun."

"Mouse? There isn't any mouse, Dick!" laughed Mary.

"Dorothy said there was," he declared.

"Yes, and I thought there was, too," went on the cook. "But it was only a piece of fur that Carlo had. It's one of the tails off Martha's fur neck-piece. She dropped it, and Carlo found it. I guess he thought it was a mouse, and I did, too, at first."

"Bow wow! Gurr-r-r-r-r!" growled the poodle dog, as he shook and tossed the fuzzy thing. And as it fell near Dick the boy looked and saw that, indeed, it was only a piece of fur, as Mary had said.

"I thought it was a mouse," said Dorothy. "And I guess Carlo did, too."

"If it had been I could have made it run back to its hole when I banged my pop gun at it!" declared Dick. "Now I guess I'll play I'm a soldier captain on a horse. I'm going to ride my Rocking Horse," he went on, as he hurried back to the playroom.

"I'll take my Sawdust Doll," said Dorothy, "and we'll have some fun."

All day long the children played, and after supper, when it was time for them to go to bed, Dick pulled his Rocking Horse out into the hall.

"Are you going to leave him there all night?" asked his mother.

"Yes," he answered. "I want to put my railroad track down in the playroom in the morning, and there isn't room if I have the Rocking Horse in there too. I'll make believe the hall is his stable."

"Then I'll not leave my Sawdust Doll out there, for she cannot sleep in a stable," said Dorothy.

Dick's mother intended to move the White Rocking Horse out of the way, for it took up too much room in the hall, but she forgot about it when callers came that evening, and, when the family went to bed, the Horse was still out near the head of the stairs that led down to the first floor.

The house became quiet, only a dim light gleaming in the upper hall, and the White Rocking Horse drew a long breath.

"Now I can be myself," he thought. "I can come to life. I wish I could see the Sawdust Doll and talk to her," he said half aloud.

"Well, here I am," and the Sawdust Doll came out of Dorothy's room.

"The little girl is asleep," went on the Sawdust Doll, "so I came out to talk to you. I want to hear all that happened in the toy hospital. I haven't had a chance to ask you since you got back."

"And I haven't had a chance to talk to you," went on the White Rocking Horse. "It is nice and quiet, now, and we can talk as long as we like; or at least until morning comes."

"It must be a funny place—that hospital," said the Sawdust Doll.

"It is," answered the Rocking Horse. "But I would much rather be here with you."

"Thank you," replied the Sawdust Doll.

Now, while the toys were thus talking together in the middle of the night, two bad men were prowling around the house where Dick and Dorothy and their father and mother lived. The two bad men were called burglars, and they wanted to get in, and take the silver knives, forks, and other things that were in the dining room, and perhaps some rings from the dresser in the room of Dorothy's mother.

And as the White Rocking Horse and the Sawdust Doll were talking together at the head of the stairs the two bad men made their way into the house by unlocking the front door with a false key one of them carried.

"Hush! Don't make a noise!" said the big burglar.

"No, we must be very quiet," said the little burglar.

But, quiet as they were, and whisper as softly as they did, the White
Rocking Horse heard them.

"Some one is coming," said the Horse to the Sawdust Doll. "We must stop talking now. We dare not talk or move if human eyes look at us, and some one is coming."

"Then I had better hurry back to Dorothy's room," said the Doll.

"Too late! They are coming up the stairs," whispered the Horse. "Stay where you are and I'll stay here too!"

So the Sawdust Doll flopped down on the carpet and the Rocking Horse remained very still and quiet right at the edge of the top step.

Up the stairs came the big burglar walking slowly and softly.

"Look out!" whispered the little burglar, who remained at the foot of the stairs. "I see something white! Look out!"

"It is only a Rocking Horse," whispered back the big burglar. "A White Rocking Horse! And a Sawdust Doll is here, too. I guess the children must have forgotten and left them in the hall. And that Sawdust Doll is just what I want. I know somebody I can give her to. I'll take her!"

The Sawdust Doll would have screamed and run away if she had dared, but she could not while the burglar was looking at her. The bad man reached out to pick up the Sawdust Doll, but his foot slipped, and, to save himself from falling, he made a grab for one of the legs of the White Rocking Horse.

Now whether the Horse kicked out; or not, I cannot say. It may be that he did, and, again, it may be that he did not. Anyhow, all of a sudden the White Horse toppled right over on top of the bad burglar, and down the stairs they went, bumpity-bump! all in a heap, right toward the little burglar standing at the foot. Down the stairs rolled the big burglar and the White Rocking Horse.

"Bang! Bing! Bung!" was the noise they made.

CHAPTER X

THE GRASS PARTY

Standing at the foot of the stairs was the little burglar. He was waiting while the big, bad man went upstairs to see if he could get any jewelry. And when the big burglar touched the White Rocking Horse, and it toppled over on him, and when both of them fell down the stairs together, making a loud noise, they fell right on top of the little burglar.

"Oh! Oh, dear! Oh, dear me!" cried the little burglar when he was struck by the big bad man and the White Rocking Horse. "Oh, what is all this? What are you doing, Jake?" he cried.

"Me? I'm not doing anything!" exclaimed the big burglar, as he went bumpity-bump along the lower hall, turning over and over in somersaults, just as the little burglar was doing.

"Not doing anything? Why, you came tumbling downstairs right on top of me!" cried the little burglar. "Why did you do that?"

"I—I couldn't help it," answered the big burglar. "That white thing you saw was a Rocking Horse, and there was a Sawdust Doll near it. I reached out to get the Doll, and the Horse stuck out his hind legs and kicked me down the stairs. That's what he did!"

"Nonsense!" exclaimed the little burglar. "A White Rocking Horse didn't kick you! A wooden horse can't kick!"

"Well, this one did," declared the burglar. "Oh, my back!"

The father and mother of Dick and Dorothy heard the noise out in the hall. So did Martha, the maid, and Mary, the cook. Dick's father sat up in bed.

"I heard a noise," said his wife.

"So did I," said Daddy. "I think everybody in the house must have heard it. Somebody, or something, fell downstairs."

"You had better look and see," said his wife. "Maybe it was burglars."

So Dick's father went out into the hall to look, and there, surely enough, were the two bad burglars. They had been all tangled up in the legs and rockers of the White Horse, and they were just getting untangled. And they were so sore and lame from having been bumped around that they did not know what to do. They were so dazed and surprised that they stood still.

And just then Patrick, the big, strong gardener, came running in from the garage, where he slept. He, too, had heard the noise in the house. And Patrick and Dick's father soon captured the two burglars, and tied them with ropes. Then a policeman came and took the two bad men away and they were locked up for a long, long time. I don't believe they are out of prison yet.

But after the two burglars had been taken away by the police, Dick's father and mother looked at the White Rocking Horse where it lay on its side in the lower hall, after having fallen downstairs.

"How do you suppose it got here?" asked Mother.

"Well, either the burglars tried to carry it off, and they slipped and fell with it, or else they stumbled over it in the dark, and it toppled downstairs with them," replied Daddy. "But it made a great racket and woke us up. If it hadn't been for the White Rocking Horse we would have been robbed of our jewelry and silver."

"What a brave Horse!" said Mother. "Wouldn't it be strange if he really kicked the burglar downstairs?" she asked her husband.

And when the burglars had been taken away, and the Horse stood up on his rockers again, Dorothy and Dick were awakened by hearing so many sounds in the house.

"What's the matter?" asked Dick, coming to the head of the stairs, and rubbing his sleepy eyes. "What's my Rocking Horse down there for?" he wanted to know.

"He fell down with the burglars," said Daddy.

[Illustration: White Rocking Horse Gives Sawdust Doll a Ride.]

"And, oh, look! Here is my Sawdust Doll out here in the hall!" cried Dorothy. "I had her in my room when I went to sleep. How did she get out here?"

"Maybe the burglars took her and were carrying her away with them when they slipped and fell downstairs with the Horse," said Daddy.

But we know that is not just how it happened, don't we? We know that the Sawdust Doll came out to talk to the White Rocking

Horse, and she could not get back when the burglars came, for she dared not move as long as they were looking at her.

For many days Dick and Dorothy had fun playing with the White Rocking Horse and the Sawdust Doll. And though, at times, the Horse and Doll wished they could see their friends in the toy store, still the two toys were very happy.

"I think something is going to happen to-morrow," said the old Jumping
Jack one night, when, in the playroom, he was talking to the Horse and
Doll. It was spring now, and the grass was green.

"What do you mean—something going to happen?" asked the White Rocking Horse, as he looked at Jack. The old jumping chap had been allowed to stay in the playroom since he had been brought from the attic on Christmas Eve.

"Dick and Dorothy are going to have a Grass Party, and you are both going to it!"

"A Grass Party!" cried the Sawdust

"What is that?" asked the White Rocking Horse.

"Well, you know what a party is," said Jack. "And a Grass Party is one out on the grass. The boy and girl from next door are coming, and there will be good things to eat, games to play and all things like that. Isn't that jolly?"

"I should say so!" cried the Rocking Horse.

"I love parties!" said the Sawdust Doll.

And the next day, when the sun was shining brightly, Dick and Dorothy had their Grass Party. Not only the little girl from next door came, but other children also. Dorothy brought out her Sawdust Doll, for whom a new apple-green dress had been made.

Dick brought his Rocking Horse to a smooth place under the trees, and he and the other boys took turns riding on the brave steed.

"Let's see where his leg was broken," asked one boy.

"Oh, you can hardly see it," Dick answered. "The toy hospital doctor fixed it so it's as good as new. But this is the leg my Horse broke when Carlo tumbled him down the steps."

"And tell us about how the two bad burglars rolled downstairs with your horse on top of them," begged Arnold, the boy from next door.

"Well, I guess only one burglar rolled down," said Dick. "But he made noise enough for two."

Then he told the story, as best he could.

While Dick and the boys rode the White Rocking Horse Dorothy and the other little girls played with their dolls. And the Sawdust Doll with the brown eyes was the most beautiful of all.

"You children do get such nice presents on your birthdays and for Christmas," said one little boy guest to Dorothy and Dick.

"I'm going to have a nice present for my birthday," said Mirabell, who lived next door to Dick and Dorothy.

"Oh, tell us!" begged the other children.

"I—I can't, for I don't know," said Mirabell. "But my mother is going to take me down to the toy store next week, and I'm going to have a nice birthday present."

And if you wish to know what the present was you may find out by

reading the next book in this series. It is called "The Story of a Lamb on Wheels," and it is the same Lamb whom the Sawdust Doll and the White Rocking Horse knew in the toy store.

After having fun at the Grass Party for some time, the children went into the house to get cake and ice cream. The Sawdust Doll and the White Rocking Horse, as well as some other dolls, were left out on the lawn by themselves.

"Oh, now we can talk," said the White Rocking Horse. "Do you think this Grass Party is any fun?"

"I had rather it were night and we could be by ourselves upstairs with the Jumping Jack," said the Sawdust Doll. "Then we could move about and have some fun."

"Well, it will soon be dark," said the Rocking Horse.

And when night came, and Dick and Dorothy were in bed, the Sawdust

Doll had a fine ride on the back of the White Rocking Horse.

The End